I0797347

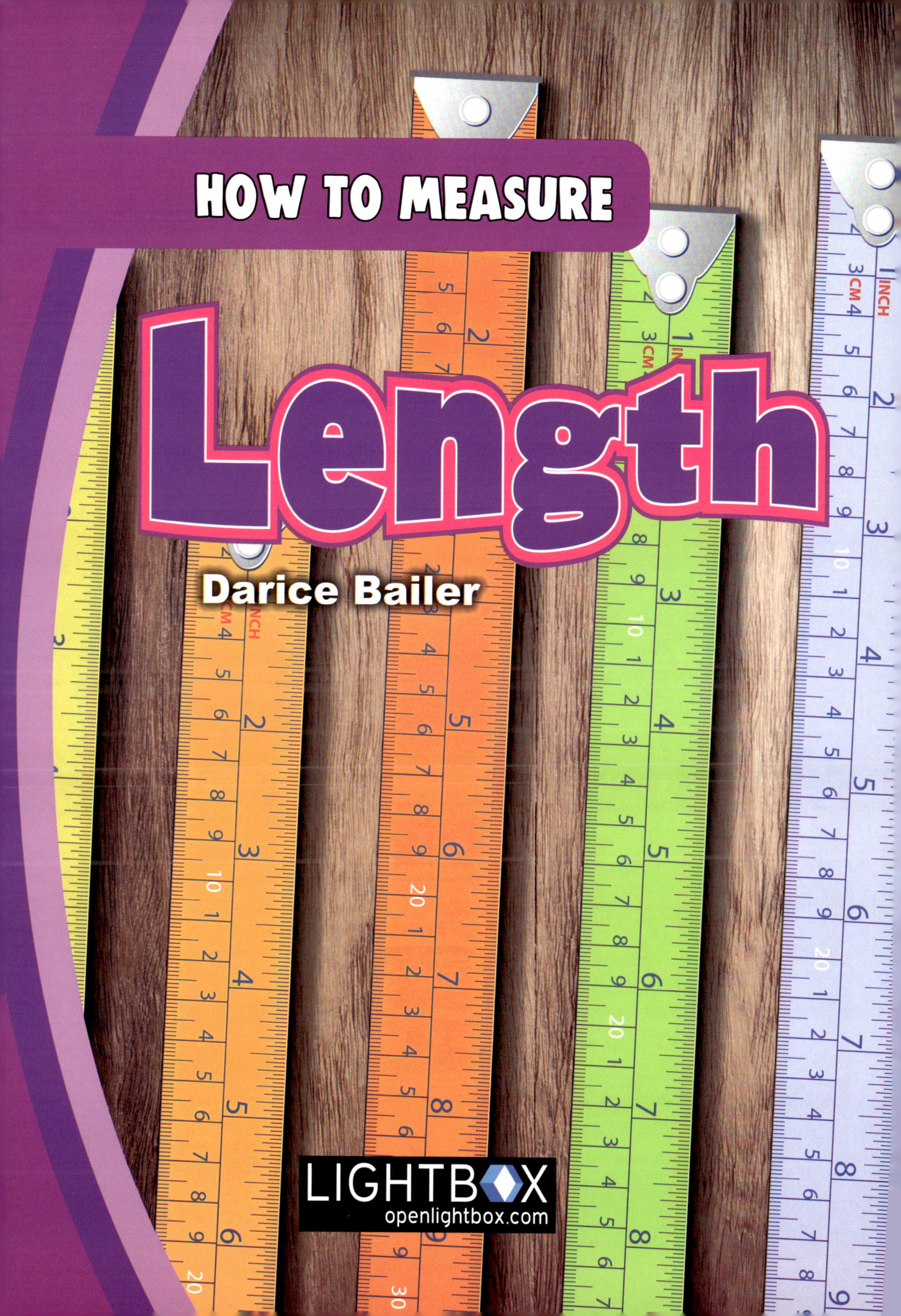

HOW TO MEASURE
Length
Darice Bailer
LIGHTBOX
openlightbox.com

Lightbox is an all-inclusive digital solution for the teaching and learning of curriculum topics in an original, groundbreaking way. Lightbox is based on National Curriculum Standards.

STANDARD FEATURES OF LIGHTBOX

AUDIO High-quality narration using text-to-speech system

ACTIVITIES Printable PDFs that can be emailed and graded

SLIDESHOWS Pictorial overviews of key concepts

VIDEOS Embedded high-definition video clips

WEBLINKS Curated links to external, child-safe resources

TRANSPARENCIES Step-by-step layering of maps, diagrams, charts, and timelines

INTERACTIVE MAPS Interactive maps and aerial satellite imagery

QUIZZES Ten multiple choice questions that are automatically graded and emailed for teacher assessment

KEY WORDS Matching key concepts to their definitions

Contents

What Is Length?

You're growing! You need a new bike and new sneakers. But what size is right? You won't know if you don't measure!

Children grow about 2.5 inches (6.4 centimeters) each year.

Measuring tells you the **distance** from point to point. Measure the length of a worm end to end. See how tall your bike is from top to bottom. That's height. See how wide you can stretch your arms. That's width. Measure how far you run from place to place. That's distance.

Most running tracks are about 1,300 feet (400 meters) around.

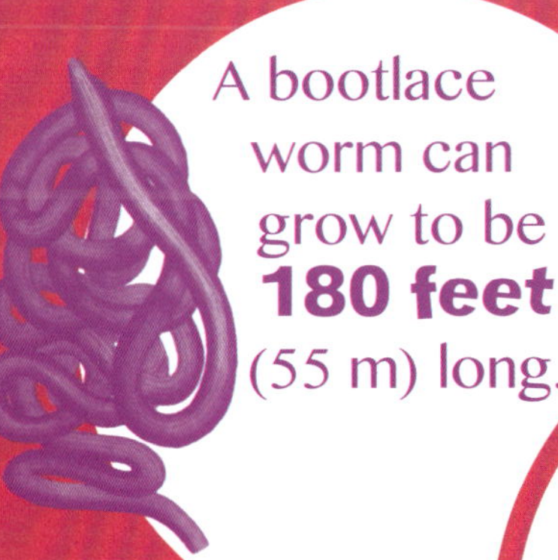

A bootlace worm can grow to be **180 feet** (55 m) long.

The world's **tallest bicycle** is more than **20 feet** (6 m) tall.

The length of a **person's armspan** is about **the same** as their height.

You can measure all these things. And you can see how much you've grown. Measuring gives you answers to all kinds of questions. Measuring helps you **compare** things. Let's measure length!

To do the activities in this book, you will need:

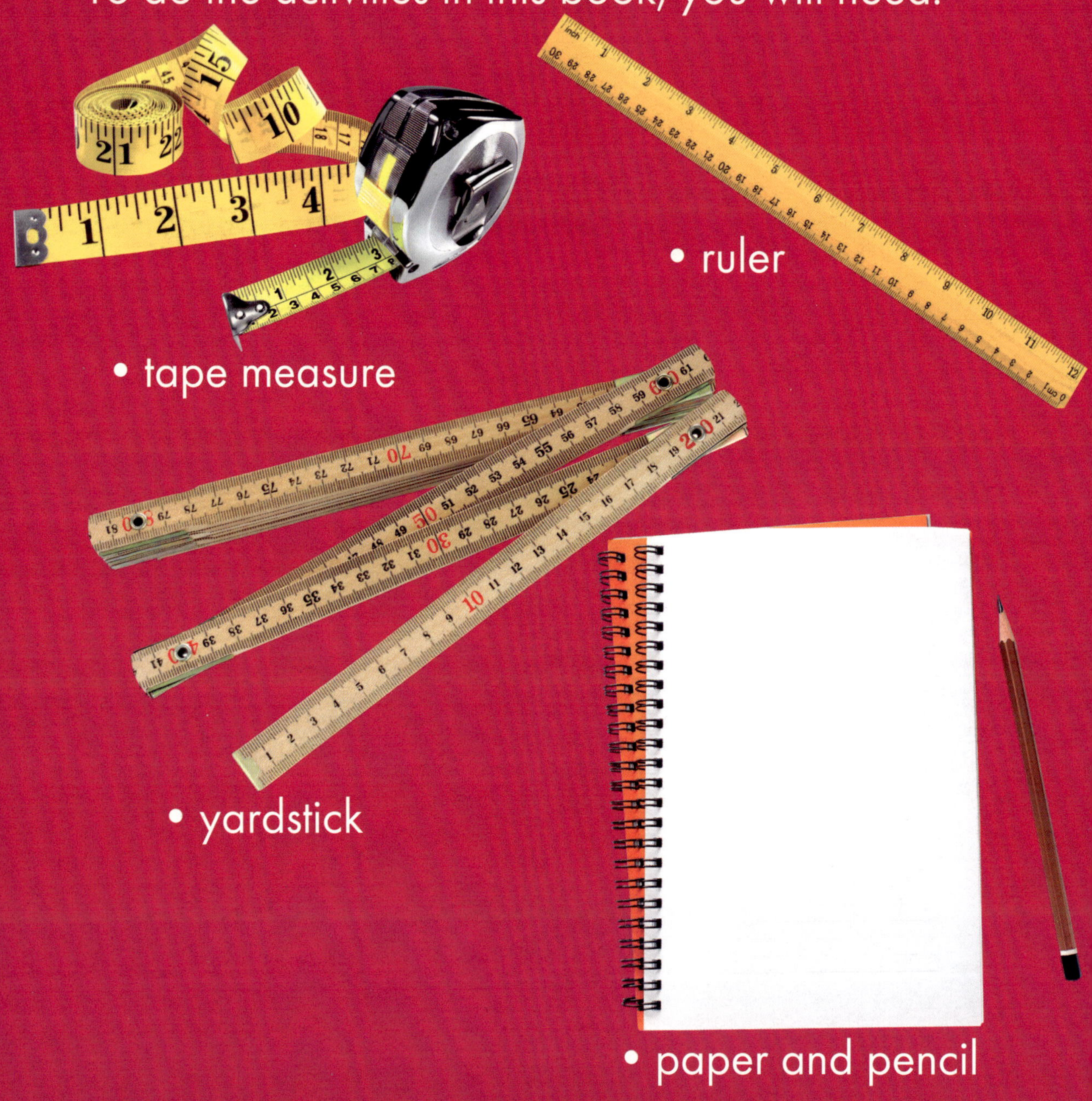

- tape measure
- ruler
- yardstick
- paper and pencil

Measuring Timeline

3000 BC The Egyptians use the cubit as a system of measurement. It is based on the distance between the elbow and the fingertips.

221 BC Shi Huang Di becomes the first emperor of China. He ensures that all provinces in China use the same measurements.

1790 President George Washington, in his first speech to Congress, says that the United States needs "**uniformity** in currency, weights and measures."

1868 Alvin J. Fellows patents the spring-click **tape measure** in the United States.

1901 The National Bureau of Standards is established by the U.S. Department of Commerce. It ensures that the same measurements are used across the country.

2016 New smart tape measures are developed. They can measure lengths in several ways, and digitally store measurements.

Starting Small

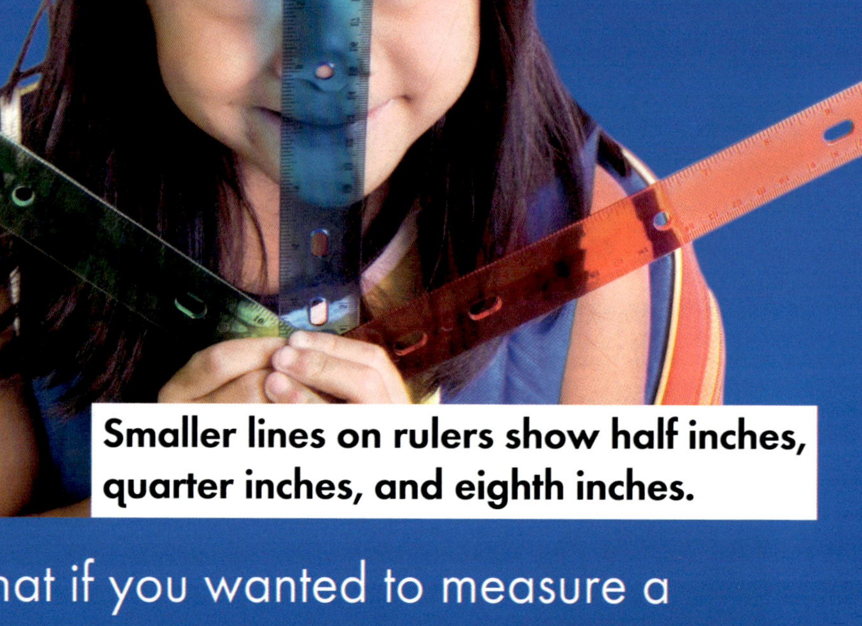

Smaller lines on rulers show half inches, quarter inches, and eighth inches.

What if you wanted to measure a small thing like your fingernail? What tool should you use? A **ruler** or a **yardstick**? A ruler measures small things like erasers, crayons, and books. A yardstick works better for longer things. It can measure the height of your bike or a grown-up.

A ruler has numbers on both sides. One side of the ruler counts from 1 to 12. This side is divided into **units** called inches. It can measure your finger in inches. There is a shorter way to write the word inch: in.

Rulers can be used to measure many objects, including school supplies.

There are 12 inches on a ruler. Twelve inches equal one foot (0.3 meter). A ruler is one foot long. That is about the length of an adult foot. Three feet make one yard. Inches, feet, and yards are units in the **U.S. customary system**.

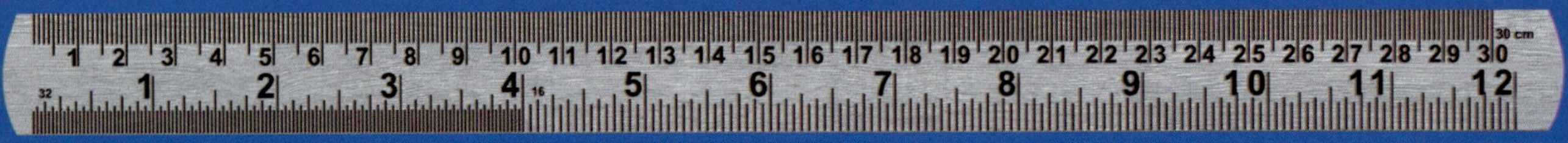

Some rulers do not show 0 where they start on the left. Others may not show 12 on the other end.

Here is a chart showing units of length.

12 inches	1 foot (0.3 m) (the length of a ruler)
3 feet	1 yard (0.9 m) (three rulers or one yardstick)
1,760 yards	1 mile (1,609 m)
5,280 feet	1 mile (1.6 kilometers)

Activity

Go on a Scavenger Hunt!

Instructions:

1. Find a bug shorter than 1 inch.
2. Find a plant taller than 1 foot.
3. Find three things inside your house that are not the same width. (One must be a person!) Measure them. Which is the widest? Thinnest?
4. Find a toy about 1 foot long.
5. Find a piece of furniture more than 1 yard long.

What else can you find to measure?

Measuring Tools

Sophie's new puppy needs a collar. Sophie needs to measure her puppy's neck. Then she can get the right collar size.

Puppies grow up very quickly. They may need more than one new collar before they are one year old.

Her friend Harry knows a ruler or yardstick would not work. He gets a tape measure instead.

The tape measure has different numbers on top and bottom. One side measures things in inches, feet, and yards. Harry and Sophie will use that side.

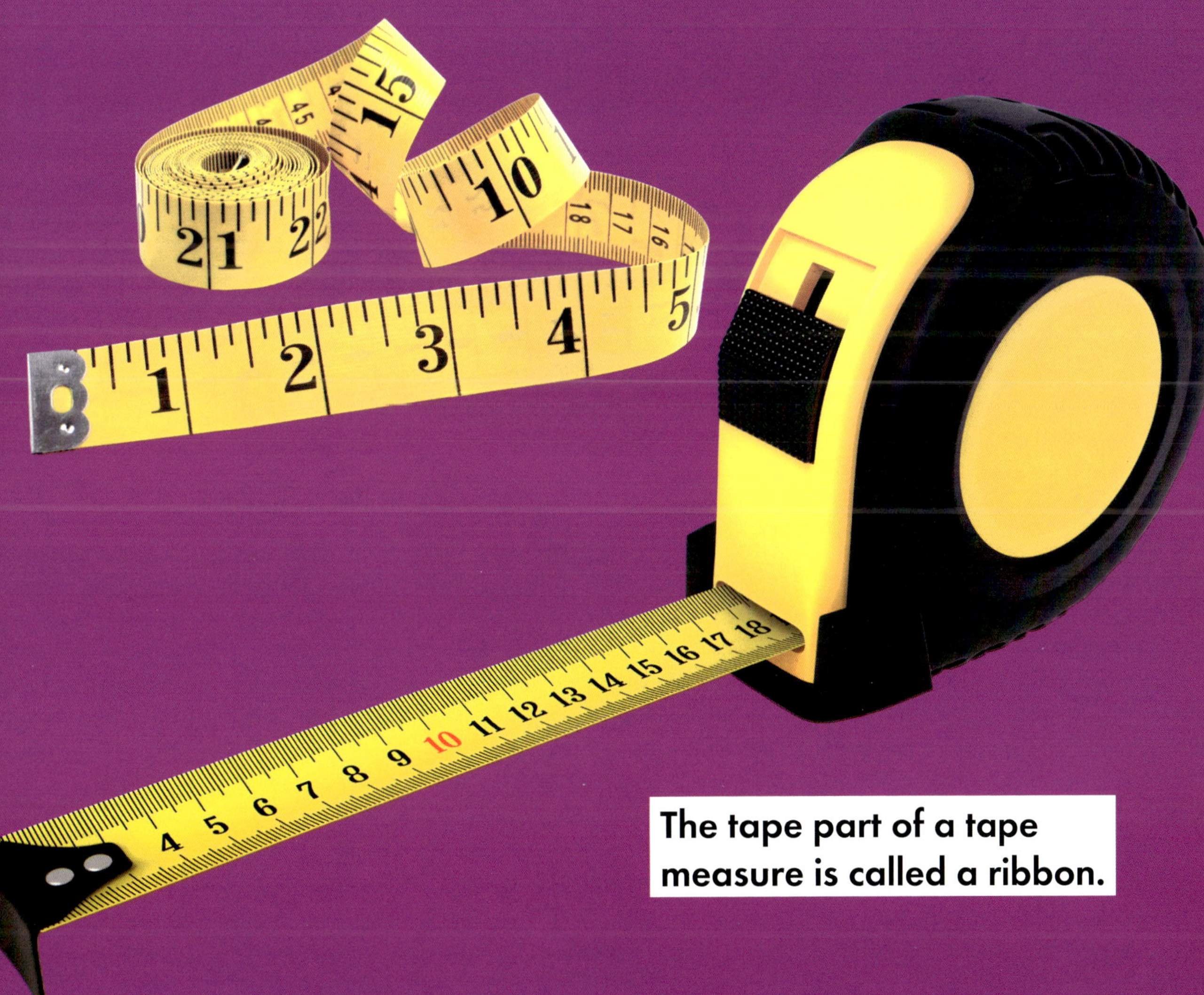

The tape part of a tape measure is called a ribbon.

Harry sees that the tape is 10 feet (3 m) long. That is as tall as his basketball hoop! Harry can measure very long or tall things with a tape measure. Harry gently places the tape around the puppy's neck to measure it. Now they know which size collar to buy.

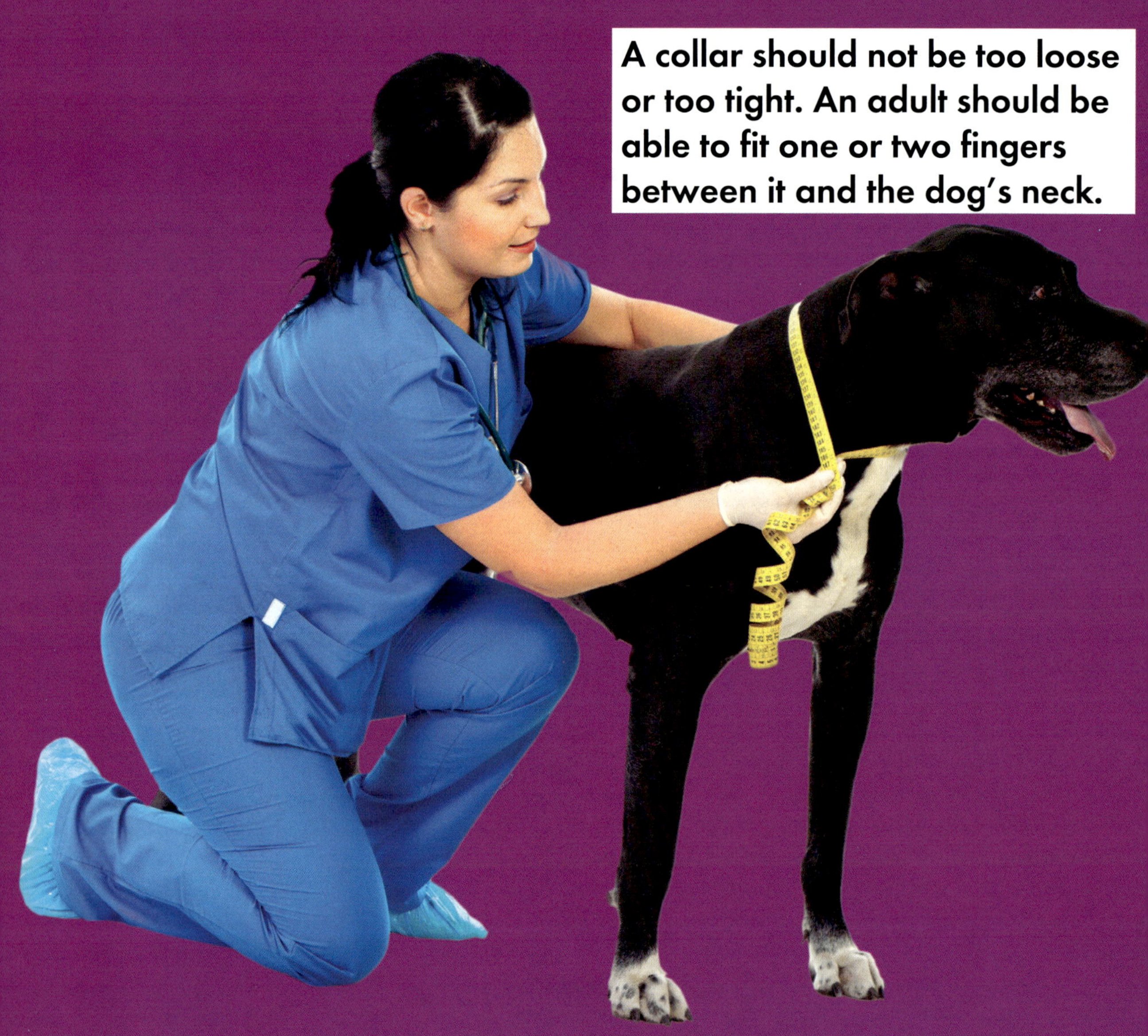

A collar should not be too loose or too tight. An adult should be able to fit one or two fingers between it and the dog's neck.

Activity

Guess the Distance

1. Find a friend. Get out a yardstick and tape measure and see how far you can jump!
2. Guess how far both of you can jump in inches.
3. Put the yardstick down on the floor. It will be the starting line!
4. Your friend should line up behind the yardstick. Then, have your friend jump!
5. Roll out the tape measure. See how far your friend jumped in inches. Write down the number.
6. Your turn!
7. How close were you to your guesses? What is the difference between your guesses and your real jumps? Who jumped furthest?

Length, Width, and Height

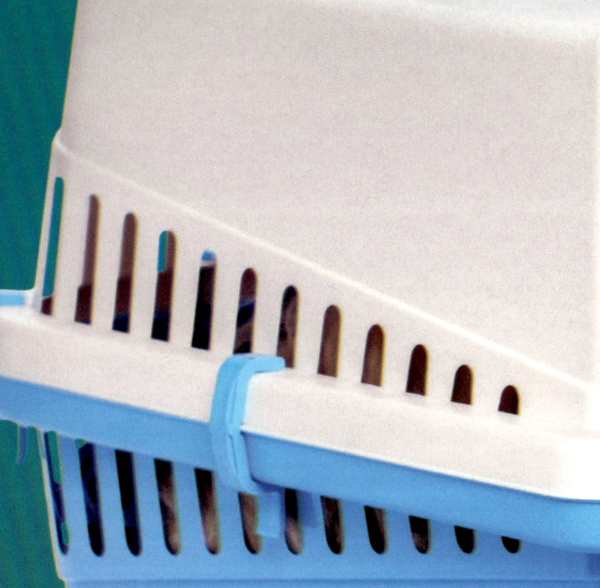

A dog carrier should be large enough for a dog to stretch out while laying down.

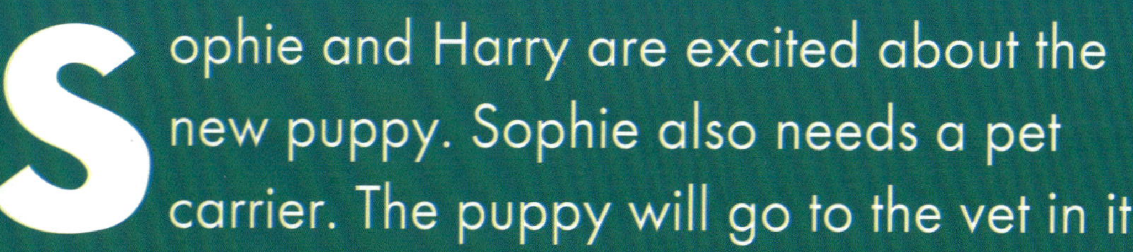

Sophie and Harry are excited about the new puppy. Sophie also needs a pet carrier. The puppy will go to the vet in it.

What size should they buy? They need to find out the carrier's length, width, and height. Sophie thinks a yardstick will help. A yardstick is three feet long.

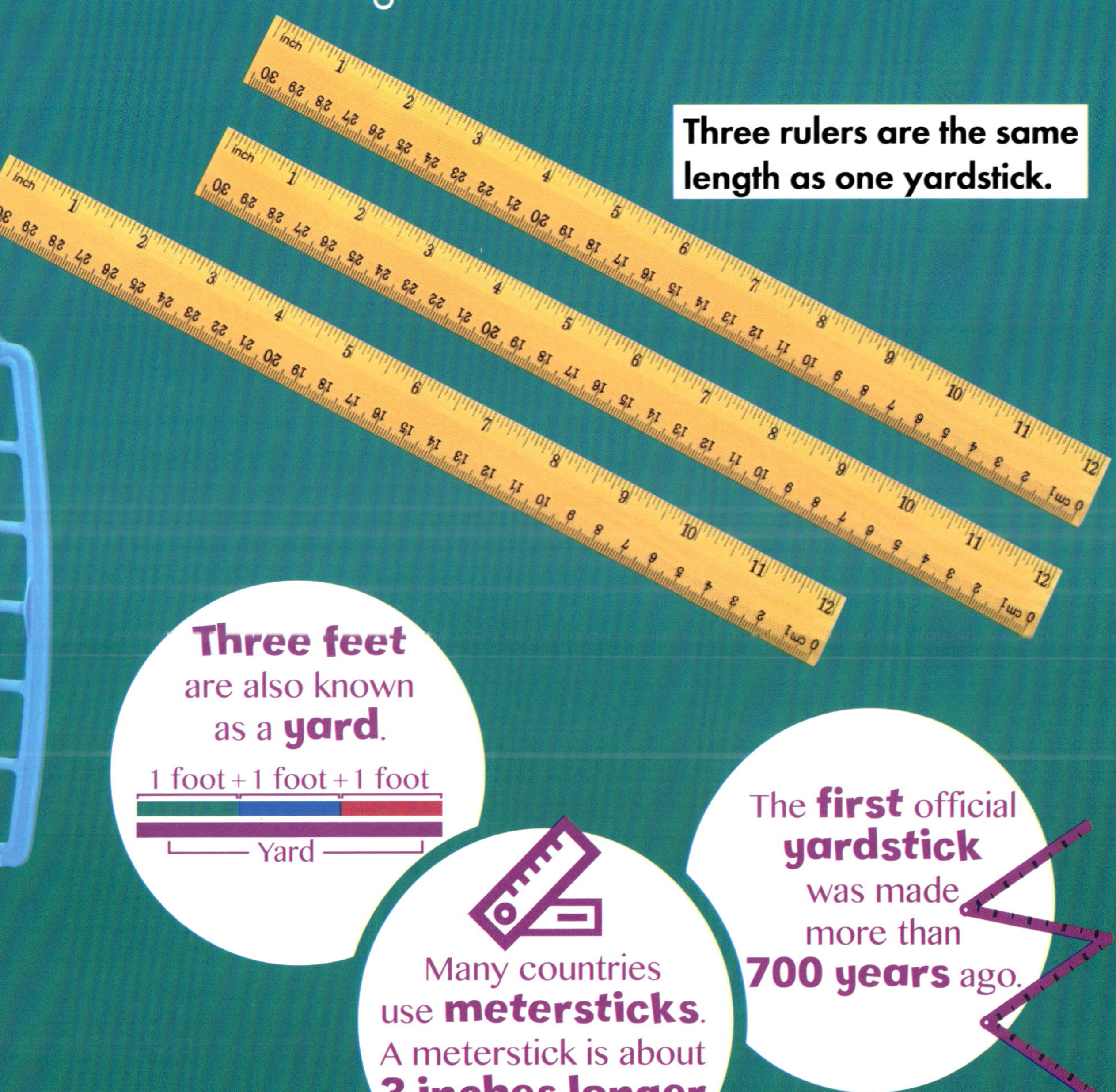

Three rulers are the same length as one yardstick.

Three feet are also known as a **yard**.

Many countries use **metersticks**. A meterstick is about **3 inches longer** than a yardstick.

The **first** official **yardstick** was made more than **700 years** ago.

Rulers, yardsticks, and tape measures have two sets of numbers. Sophie and Harry used inches and feet before. This time, they want to use the other numbers.

The other numbers are in the **metric system.** The metric system measures with units called centimeters and meters.

The metric system counts in tens. One hundred centimeters equal one meter. That is about 39 inches, or a little longer than a yard. There is a shorter way to write centimeters: cm.

What can you do with a ruler, a yardstick, and a tape measure? Like Harry and Sophie, you can measure all sorts of things. And you can measure in different ways!

Today, most tape measures are between 12 feet (3.6 m) and 100 feet (30.5 m) long.

Activity

Inches and Centimeters

Instructions:
Use a yardstick or tape measure to help you answer the questions.

1 Height
Sophie thinks 36 inches is too tall for a carrier.
They need one 12 inches shorter.
How many inches do they need?
How many feet is that?
How many centimeters are in that many feet?

2 Width
They need a carrier at least 1 foot wide.
How many centimeters are in 1 foot?

3 Length
The carrier should be half a yard long from front to back.
How many inches is half a yard?
How many centimeters is this?

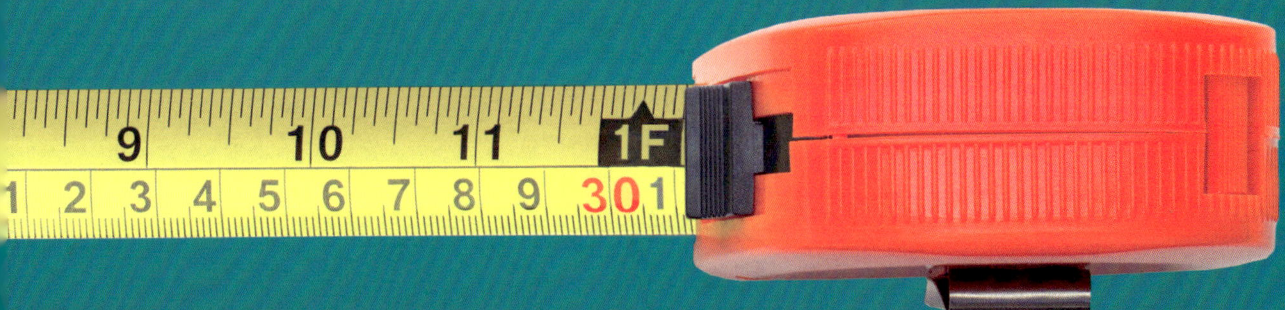

Record-Setting Lengths and Heights

There are many record-setting landmarks in the United States. Some of these are the tallest or longest in the nation, or even in the world.

Canada

United States

Montana

Oregon

Idaho

Wyoming

Utah

Nevada

California

Pacific Ocean

Mexico

Denali

Denali National Park, Alaska

Alaska has the seven highest mountains in the United States. Denali, the tallest, is 20,320 feet (6,194 m)above sea level.

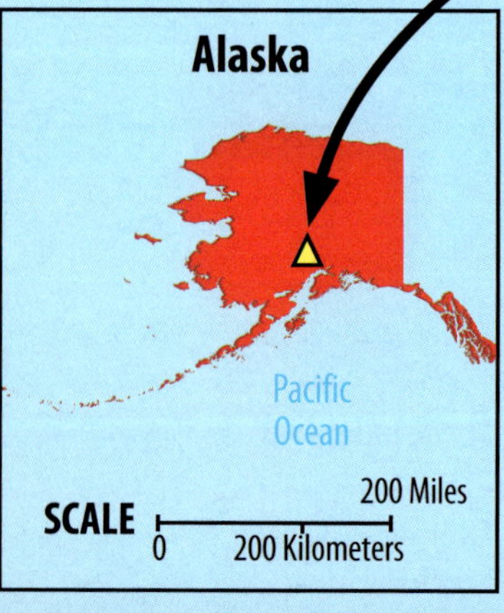

Missouri River
The Missouri River, the longest river in the United States, runs for 2,341 miles (3,767 km) from Montana to the Mississippi River north of St. Louis, Missouri.
One World Trade Center
New York City, New York
At 1,776 feet (541 m) tall, One World Trade Center is the tallest building in the United States.
Talladega Superspeedway
Lincoln, Alabama
Talladega Superspeedway is the biggest NASCAR track. The course is 2.66 miles (4.3 km) long.
North Dakota
South Dakota
Minnesota
Wisconsin
Michigan
Nebraska
Iowa
Illinois
Indiana
Ohio
Kansas
Missouri
Kentucky
West Virginia
Virginia
Pennsylvania
New York
Maine
Vermont
New Hampshire
Massachusetts
Rhode Island
Connecticut
New Jersey
Delaware
Maryland
Tennessee
North Carolina
South Carolina
Alabama
Georgia
Florida
LEGEND
United States
Other Countries
Denali National Park
City
River
Water
N
W
E
S
SCALE
0
250 Miles
250 Kilometers

1 How many feet are in a yard?

2 How many inches does a ruler measure?

3 When was the first official yardstick made?

4 What does measuring something tell you?

5 What is the longest river in the United States?

6 What is the tape part of a tape measure called?

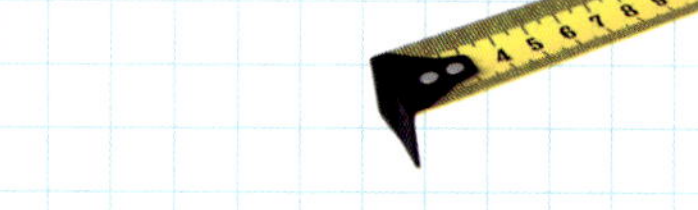

7 What did the U.S. Department of Commerce establish in 1901?

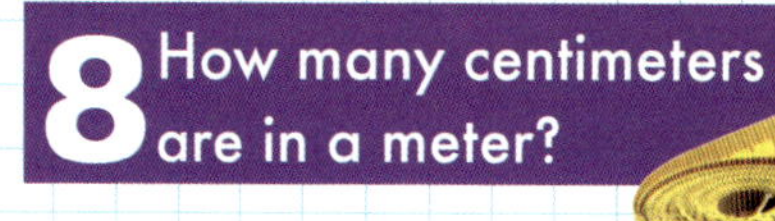

8 How many centimeters are in a meter?

9 About how many inches do children grow each year?

10 Which state has the seven highest mountains in the United States?

wers: 1. Three **2.** Twelve **3.** More than 700 years ago **4.** The distance from point to point
he Missouri River **6.** The ribbon **7.** The National Bureau of Standards **8.** 100 **9.** 2.5 **10.** Alaska

Key Words

compare: to look at differences and similarities in a thing

distance: the length between two places

metric system: a way to measure things based on the number ten using units such as centimeters and meters

NASCAR: National Association for Stock Car Auto Racing

ruler: a long piece of plastic, wood, or metal that measures inches or centimeters

tape measure: a long piece of fabric or metal that unrolls to measure long things

uniformity: being the same

units: standard amounts that are used to measure things

U.S. customary system: units of measurement typically used in the United States such as cups, quarts, miles, feet, and inches

yardstick: a thin, long tool 36 inches long used for measuring

Index

LIGHTBOX

SUPPLEMENTARY RESOURCES

Click on the plus icon ⊕ found in the bottom left corner of each spread to open additional teacher resources.

- Download and print the book's quizzes and activities
- Access curriculum correlations
- Explore additional web applications that enhance the Lightbox experience

LIGHTBOX DIGITAL TITLES

Packed full of integrated media

VIDEOS

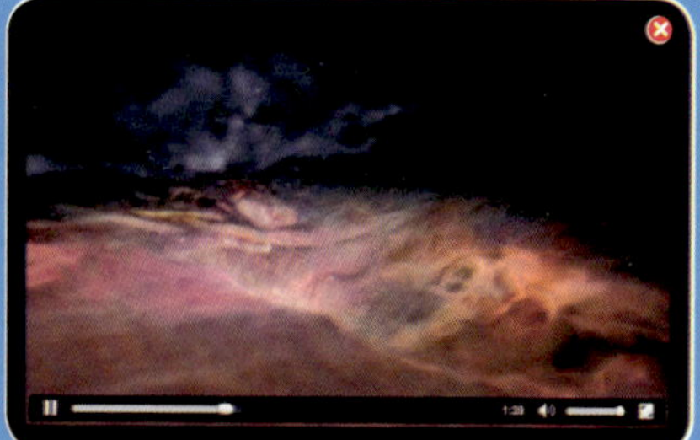

INTERACTIVE MAPS

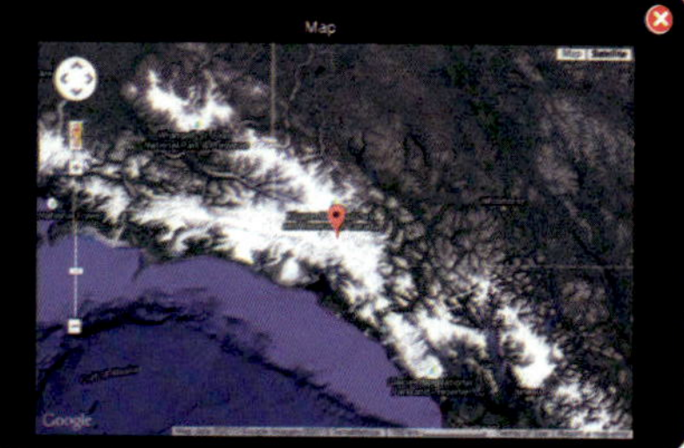

WEBLINKS

SLIDESHOWS

QUIZZES

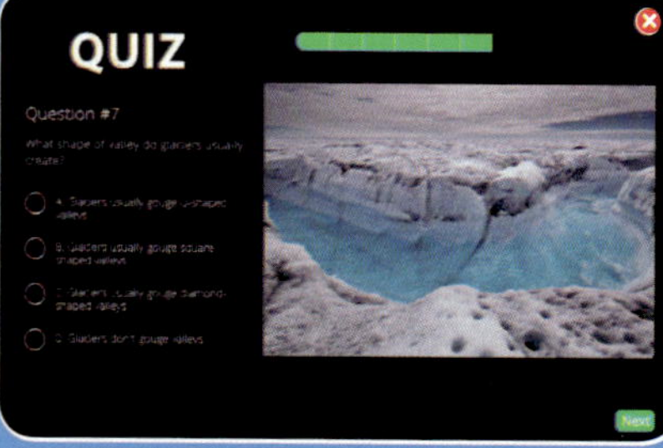

OPTIMIZED FOR

- ✓ TABLETS
- ✓ WHITEBOARDS
- ✓ COMPUTERS
- ✓ AND MUCH MORE!

Published by Smartbook Media Inc. 350 5th Avenue, 59th Floor New York, NY 10118
Website: www.openlightbox.com

012018
120517

Library of Congress Control Number: 2017960146

ISBN 978-1-5105-3626-5 (hardcover)
ISBN 978-1-5105-3627-2 (multi-user eBook)

Printed in the Brainerd, Minnesota, United States
1 2 3 4 5 6 7 8 9 0 22 21 20 19 18

First published by Cherry Lake in 2014.

Project Coordinator: John Willis
Designer: Ana María Vidal

Every reasonable effort has been made to trace ownership and to obtain permission to reprint copyright material. The publisher would be pleased to have any errors or omissions brought to its attention so that they may be corrected in subsequent printings.

The publisher acknowledges Alamy, Getty Images, iStock, and Dreamstime as the primary image suppliers for this title.